ECO-DISASTERS

RISING SEAS

MIAMI, FLORIDA

by Kevin Blake

Consultants: Dr. George A. Maul
Professor of Oceanography
Florida Institute of Technology
Melbourne, Florida

Colin Polsky, PhD
Director, Center for Environmental Studies
Florida Atlantic University
Boca Raton, Florida

BEARPORT
PUBLISHING

New York, New York

Credits

Publisher: Kenn Goin
Editor: Jessica Rudolph
Creative Director: Spencer Brinker
Photo Researcher: Editorial Directions, Inc.

Library of Congress Cataloging-in-Publication Data

Names: Blake, Kevin, 1978– author.
Title: Rising seas : Miami, Florida / by Kevin Blake.
Description: New York, New York : Bearport Publishing Company, Inc., [2018] |
    Series: Eco-disasters | Includes bibliographical references and index. |
    Identifiers: LCCN 2017015977 (print) | LCCN 2017020078 (ebook) | ISBN
    9781684022823 (ebook) | ISBN 9781684022281 (library)
Subjects: LCSH: Sea level—Florida—Miami—Juvenile literature. | Climatic
    changes—Florida—Miami—Juvenile literature. | Global
    warming—Florida—Miami—Juvenile literature.
Classification: LCC GC90.U5 (ebook) | LCC GC90.U5 B53 2018 (print) | DDC
    363.34/9—dc23
LC record available at https://lccn.loc.gov/2017015977

For more information, write to Bearport Publishing Company, Inc., 45 West 21st Street, Suite 3B, New York, New York 10010. Printed in the United States of America.

10 9 8 7 6 5 4 3 2 1

Contents

Water Everywhere

Strange things are happening in the city of Miami. On a bright sunny morning, a man walks across a flooded neighborhood park while carrying his small dog. Nearby, a woman looks out her apartment window to see a stream of water flowing down the street past her front door. A restaurant owner suddenly finds a giant puddle where his outdoor tables used to be.

The number of days every year that Miami floods has been increasing.

Water is part of the Miami landscape.

These odd scenes of flooding are occurring more often in Miami, Florida. For many years, millions of Americans have lived in and visited this **vibrant** city located along Biscayne Bay and the Atlantic Ocean. Now, however, it seems like the ocean is slowly swallowing the city. As scientist Harold Wanless warns, "Miami, as we know it today, is doomed."

The Miami **metropolitan area** is the eighth largest in the United States. More than six million people live there.

Changing Wetlands

Miami's fight against creeping water isn't new. In fact, Miami used to be part of the Everglades, one giant **wetland** area that covered nearly all of South Florida. It was a perfect home for alligators, birds, and other wetland animals. The Everglades was a difficult place for people to live. However, for thousands of years, Native Americans such as the Seminoles made it their home.

Alligators and other swamp animals live in the Florida Everglades.

A Seminole village in the Everglades in the 1800s

In the early 1900s, businessmen started changing the region so it would be suitable for large numbers of people to live there. They drained much of the water from South Florida and sent it into the Atlantic Ocean and the Gulf of Mexico. By 1920, more than 200 miles (322 km) of **canals** were dug to **divert** the water and dry out the land. It worked. With the swamp cleared out, towns like Miami grew and became popular **tourist** destinations.

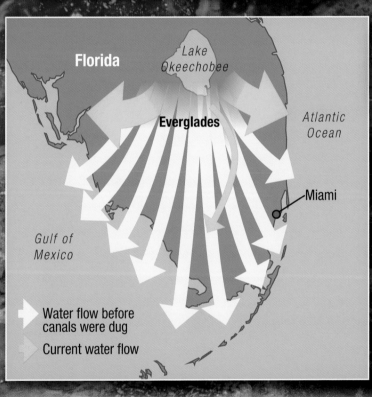

Florida

Lake Okeechobee

Everglades

Atlantic Ocean

Gulf of Mexico

Miami

Water flow before canals were dug

Current water flow

Much of the water from the Everg used to flow south toward Miami. After the canals were dug, most o water flowed east and west.

Before it was drained, the Everglades covered more than 4,000 square miles (10,360 sq km). That's bigger than the states of Rhode Island and Delaware combinec

An Everglades canal

A Hotter Planet

The canals were enough to keep the water out 100 years ago, but more needs to be done today. Why? The world's **climate** is changing. Since the canals were dug, there has been major damage to the environment.

The climate of Miami—like the rest of the world—is changing.

Pollution created by factories, cars, and other manmade objects has led to significant changes to Earth's atmosphere. The pollution causes the atmosphere to trap more heat than it did before. The world's temperature is now more than 1°F hotter than it was 100 years ago. That might not seem like a lot, but even that small change can create serious changes in Earth's fragile environment.

Factories can pump gases into the air, such as methane and carbon dioxide, which cause climate change.

Some scientists think Earth's average temperature could increase by as much as 1.8°F to 7.2°F by the year 2100.

Melting Ice, Rising Seas

A warmer planet can lead to disaster because of the large sheets of ice on areas of land such as Greenland and Antarctica. As temperatures rise, the ice melts and the water spills into the surrounding oceans. This causes the **sea level** to rise. Some scientists worry that if the planet continues to warm, the seas could rise by as much as 3.2 to 6.6 feet (1 to 2 m) by 2100.

A polar bear on an iceberg near the coast of Greenland

The sea level around Miami has been rising by about 9 inches (23 cm) every century.

Why are rising water levels such a big problem for Miami? Parts of the city are only about 6 feet (1.8 m) above sea level. As sea levels rise, the flooding risk in the city increases. If sea levels rose 2 feet (0.6 m), sections of Miami would be covered by salt water. At 4 feet (1.2 m), the average 12-year-old child would be up to his or her neck in ocean water. At 6 feet (1.8 m), much of Miami would be underwater.

A man kayaks along a flooded Miami street.

Six Directions

Miami is at risk for flooding not only because it sits at a low **elevation**. Water comes into the city from six directions: north, south, east, and west, as well as from the sky and the ground below! South Florida is a peninsula. It's surrounded by ocean water on three sides. Some water from the Everglades drains toward the city from the north. A rainy climate pours down water from the sky.

Miami experiences many thunderstorms between May and October.

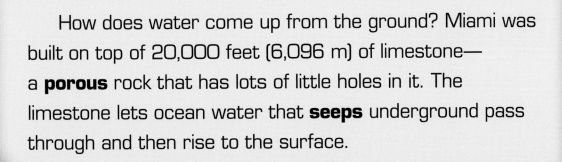

How does water come up from the ground? Miami was built on top of 20,000 feet (6,096 m) of limestone— a **porous** rock that has lots of little holes in it. The limestone lets ocean water that **seeps** underground pass through and then rise to the surface.

The limestone under Miami is made up, in part, of ancient deposits of **coral** and clamshells.

Floods!

Rising water has already had serious **consequences** for Miami. Starting in 2009, the city began to experience frequent floods—even on sunny days. Pools of salt water would suddenly rise from the ground, and streams of water would block off entrances to buildings or entire streets. Some new puddles were as big as ponds!

Cars drive through a flooded street. Salty floodwaters are often corrosive—they can wear away the paint and even the metal on cars.

The floods are often more than just annoyances—they can also be dangerous. Sometimes the water running through the street isn't clean. The water can contain **sewage** from leaky sewer pipes that run beneath Miami's roads, or even garbage from the streets. "It's horrible," one Miami resident said. "Sometimes the water actually smells."

A flooded street littered with garbage

The sewage water can contain harmful **bacteria** that may make people and animals sick.

Harming the Everglades

The rising ocean water can also **contaminate** the city's drinking water. Miami gets much of its drinking water from the freshwater Everglades north of the city. However, as fresh water is removed from the wetland area for drinking, ocean water slowly creeps north through the underground porous limestone and pushes salt into the fresh water. This makes the Everglades' water unsafe to drink for the millions of Floridians who depend on it.

Certain towns near Miami, like Hallandale Beach, have had to close some of their drinking wells because they're filling up with salty water.

Millions of people in South Florida depend on fresh water from the Everglades.

Salt water in the Everglades also threatens the **native** plants, mammals, and birds that depend on fresh water. Scientists are already noticing that the freshwater sawgrass is dying and being replaced by mangrove trees that can survive in salty water.

Sawgrass (above) is being replaced by mangroves (right).

A Serious Disease

Flooding around a city can have other terrible consequences—including the spread of diseases. For instance, because mosquitoes **breed** in standing water, the extra water pooling around the city may result in more mosquitoes that can spread **viruses** to people.

Newly born mosquitoes in standing water

In 2016, mosquitoes in Miami began spreading Zika, a particularly dangerous disease. Zika can create serious problems for pregnant women and **fetuses**. To fight back against the mosquitoes, local government officials instructed people to drain standing water wherever they found it. That's not easy in a city that's often flooding.

The *Aedes aegypti* mosquito spreads Zika.

Babies born with Zika can have smaller than normal heads and brains. This condition is called microcephaly (mye-kroh-SEPH-uh-lee).

Babies with microcephaly can have trouble swallowing, speaking, and learning.

King Tide

Miami's water problems are at their worst during "King **Tide**." This is when the moon is closest to Earth and causes the sea to rise to its highest point. The King Tide on November 14, 2016, was no exception. Ocean water spilled into Miami, spreading water throughout the city. The flooding even dumped an octopus in the middle of a parking garage!

During the King Tide on November 14, 2016, the moon was the closest it had been to Earth in almost 70 years.

The moon's **gravitational** pull causes the ocean's tides to rise and fall.

The rising seas mean that people in some Miami neighborhoods may have to move to other sections of the city or even to other towns. "There's no keeping the water out," worries Philip Stoddard, the mayor of South Miami. "So ultimately, this area has to **depopulate**. What I want to work toward is a slow and graceful depopulation, rather than a sudden . . . one." Others are busy trying to find solutions to save the city.

Floods can make walking through the street difficult.

Pumping the Water Out

One solution is to use pumps to suck the water off streets and shoot it into nearby Biscayne Bay. The city of Miami Beach, located on an island near Miami, has begun its plan to spend $300 million dollars to build 60 giant underground pumps.

Miami Beach workers prepare to install a new water pump.

Each pump can push out 14,000 gallons (53,000 l) of water per minute!

There are problems with the pumps, however. First, if sea levels continue to rise, the electric pumps themselves may become so flooded that they won't work properly. Second, the pumps often shoot dirty water—polluted by sewage and other waste—into Biscayne Bay, where many sea animals live and people like to swim and surf!

Biscayne Bay, one of the reasons people love Miami, may be unusable if it becomes too polluted.

Building Up

Another idea is to actually raise parts of the city so floodwaters do not interfere with residents' everyday lives. "Elevation is a key aspect of our plan," says Bruce Mowry, an **engineer** working for Miami Beach. "Considering what Mother Nature is putting on us with sea-level rise, we may have to change our **culture** in order to survive."

This street might have stayed dry if it were raised higher above the ground.

Construction workers have already rebuilt some streets around Miami and nearby towns to raise them by more than 3 feet (0.9 m). This has created some strange situations where stores and restaurants are actually below street level. However, even a few extra feet can help roads stay clear of water during high tide events.

This street was raised higher so cars can safely pass through during floods.

Some South Florida towns only allow new buildings to be constructed on elevated ground so they will stay dry during a flood.

Miami Tomorrow

Pumps and raised streets are just temporary solutions. If the oceans rise by up to 6 feet (1.8 m) as some scientists predict, neither solution will help Miami to survive. At that rate, Miami and much of South Florida will be underwater. Without a long-term solution, millions of people will have to move to another area.

Miami's beaches could disappear completely if water levels continue to rise.

While Miami is in particular trouble, other coastal cities, such as New Orleans and New York City, are also threatened by rising seas.

The only real solution for Miami is to slow climate change and the rising oceans before it's too late. That means **conserving** energy, using less water, and limiting pollution. With everyone working together, the wonderful city of Miami may be saved.

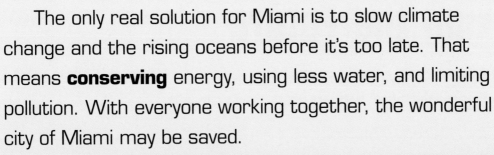

Reducing pollution by using clean energy, such as solar power, can help fight climate change.

Fixing the Future

Fighting climate change is the best way to save Miami and other coastal cities. Here are ways people can help.

An electric car

New Cars

Old cars and trucks create a lot of exhaust by burning gasoline. Driving new fuel-efficient and electric cars help Earth by creating less pollution that's harmful to the environment.

Other Forms of Energy

Using **renewable** energy from sources such as the sun or wind prevents the release of greenhouse gases. These gases, such as carbon dioxide and methane, trap warm air in the atmosphere and raise Earth's temperature.

Wind farms can create energy without causing significant air pollution.

Many climate change parades are held on April 22, which is Earth Day.

Getting Involved

People can volunteer or donate money to organizations that help the environment, such as the Sierra Club or groups that are focused on saving Florida, like the Florida Climate Institute.

Being Heard

- People can write to their elected leaders to tell them they are concerned about climate change and the future of cities like Miami.

- Another way people can let their representatives know about their concerns about climate change is to take part in rallies, parades, and protests that demand laws be passed to protect the environment.

Congress can pass laws to try to protect the environment and slow climate change.

Glossary

bacteria (bak-TEER-ee-uh) tiny life forms that can only be seen under a microscope; some bacteria can cause disease, but some are helpful in keeping humans and animals healthy

breed (BREED) to produce young

canals (kuh-NALZ) channels that are dug across land, often to transport water

climate (KLYE-mit) patterns of weather over a long period of time

consequences (KAHN-sih-*kwen*-siz) the results of something that happened earlier

conserving (kuhn-SURV-ing) not wasting

contaminate (kuhn-TAM-uh-nayt) to make something dirty or polluted

coral (KORE-uhl) hard material that is made up of the skeletons of small creatures found in shallow tropical waters

culture (KUHL-chur) the customs and traditions shared by a group of people

depopulate (dee-PAHP-yoo-layt) to reduce the population of an area

divert (dye-VURT) to change the direction of something

elevation (el-uh-VAY-shun) an area's height above sea level

engineer (en-juh-NEER) someone who designs and builds things such as machines, bridges, vehicles, and roads

fetuses (FEE-tus-iz) unborn offspring still in the mother's womb

gravitational (grav-uh-TAY-shun-uhl) having to do with the force that pulls things toward Earth, the sun, or other bodies in space

metropolitan area (met-roh-PAHL-uh-tuhn AIR-ee-uh) a large city and the suburbs and smaller cities that surround it

native (NAY-tiv) living or growing naturally in a particular place

porous (PORE-uss) full of holes that allow liquids or gases to pass through

renewable (rih-NOO-uh-buhl) able to be replaced by natural processes

sea level (SEE LEV-uhl) the average height of the sea's surface

seeps (SEEPZ) passes, flows, or oozes slowly through a small opening

sewage (SOO-ij) liquid and solid wastes that go down drains

tide (TIDE) movement of an ocean or other large body of water toward or away from the shore

tourist (TOOR-ist) someone who travels to and visits places for fun

vibrant (VYE-bruhnt) exciting, fun

viruses (VYE-ruhss-iz) tiny germs that can only be seen with powerful microscopes; they can invade cells and cause diseases

wetland (WET-land) marshy land; land where the soil is very moist or wet

Bibliography

Allen, Greg. "As Waters Rise, Miami Beach Builds Higher Streets and Political Willpower," *npr.org* (May 10, 2016).

Gillis, Justin. "Flooding of Coast, Caused by Global Warming, Has Already Begun," *The New York Times* (September 3, 2016).

Kolbert, Elizabeth. "The Siege of Miami," *The New Yorker* (December 2015).

Read More

Orme, Helen. *Climate Change (Earth in Danger).* New York: Bearport (2009).

Simon, Seymour. *Global Warming.* New York: HarperCollins (2013).

Learn More Online

To learn more about Miami's rising seas, visit
www.bearportpublishing.com/EcoDisasters

Index

About the Author

Kevin Blake has written many nonfiction books for kids.
He lives in Providence, Rhode Island, with his
wife, Melissa, son, Sam, and daughter, Ilana. He's
visited South Florida often—and hopes people
find a way to stop Miami's rising seas!